The Mystery of Two Creations

Emmanuel J. Charles

ISBN 978-1-63874-294-4 (paperback)
ISBN 978-1-63874-295-1 (digital)

Christian Faith Publishing, Inc.
832 Park Avenue
Meadville, PA 16335
www.christianfaithpublishing.com

Printed in the United States of America

Contents

Preface

─────────── ❧ ───────────

The Story of This Book

I am not a scientist, philosopher, or a theologian, but my book contains all three elements.

It was during September 2020 that I came back from work and had some time to listen to the political news. Instead, my attention fell on the Hoover Institution discussing Darwin's theory of evolution with Peter Robinson as moderator, along with Dr. Stephen Meyer, Dr. David Berlinski, and Dr. David Galernter. The topic was "Has Darwinism really failed?" All three experts agreed that the theory of evolution should be dismissed, dissected, developed, or replaced.

What I heard was disturbing. None of these scientists approved the theory of evolution. I was praying and asking God if this theory is not true, then the answer lies somewhere. Immediately, I went to the book of Genesis chapter 1 and read the whole chapter. It was the same old story which I have read from my childhood numerous times. As I was seeking the answer, three to seven days passed and on one of the Wednesdays during my fasting and prayer time, I heard the account of Elijah challenging the people of Israel, stating, "How long will you waiver between two opinions?" If God be God, follow Him and if Baal, follow him.

That evening I was troubled and asked God how long my generation will waiver between two opinions. If God be God, follow Him; and if science, follow it. Again, I went to Genesis 1. Immediately, the Rhema, the revelation of God, came to me, and my eyesight fixed on

Genesis 1:2. There, the earth existed before the day one account of His creation that is in Genesis 1:3.

This was a big surprise for me because the creation of the earth was missing from the creation account during the six-day period. So, I realized that the creation of the earth is from Genesis 1:1, and if the earth existed, then the solar system must be present. I understood that without the presence of the sun, the earth cannot rotate on its axis and go on its orbit around the sun. Also, this theory brought me to the conclusion that if darkness covers the earth, that means the sun is not able to put forth light as it always does. That is how I came to know that darkness engulfed the sun and stars.

I was happy that God showed me this truth to unlock the hidden mystery of creation according to Genesis 1. I was always interested in knowing the truth because John 8:32 says, "You shall know the truth, and the truth shall set you free." It is not only knowing and understanding the truth in spiritual matters but also in day-to-day life. This world is full of delusions and deceptions; therefore, you will eliminate the problems by finding the solution in advance before you fall as a prey and face consequences.

Also, when the "Rhema," revelation of God, comes, we should be able to understand it. That is only possible for those whose hearts are regenerated by the power of the Holy Spirit and know Him personally. In other words, be born again and renew your mind with His word (Bible) daily.

Many times, we think it is a metaphor, but it is literal especially when it comes to Genesis 1:1, 1:2, and 1:3–31.

Chapter One

❧

The Earth Is 4.5 Billion Years Old and Had a Blackout That Remained for Sixty-Five Million Years

There is a conflict raging between two thoughts; they are the creationists and the scientific community (evolutionists). It basically comes down to God or science. The creationists on God's side say that the earth was created with plants, animals, and human beings in six days and the earth is six thousand years old. On the other hand, the scientific community says that the earth is 4.5 billion years old and the plants, animals, and humans evolved to its present form by a theory called evolution.

According to the scientific community, most scientists believe it is heresy to deny evolution, and those who are found guilty will be disbarred from their circles and will be left without grant money for their scientific research. It will go farther than that, they will also lose their jobs and will be ostracized.

The church establishment believed that if anybody dared to speak contrary to God's Word, they would be punished with the death penalty. For example, Giordano Bruno who believed and carried the work of heliocentric theory discovered by Nicolas Copernicus long ago was burned alive at the stake. The great scientist Galileo had to apologize and renounce his finding that the earth revolves around the sun and the earth is not the center of the universe.

The truth of the matter is that we have lost free speech and free expression among the creationists and the scientific community. The question of our time is then who is right and who is wrong? I hope my new discovery will bridge both groups for the betterment of humans and the world.

Timeline

Genesis 1:1—First Creation: The formation of the Earth during the **Precambrian** Era 4.5 billion years ago.

Genesis 1:2—The earth remained without form for sixty-five million years. Beginning of the Tertiary Period, **Cenozoic Era**, and the end of the Cretaceous Period, **Mesozoic Era**.

Genesis 1:3—Second creation/rearranging in six days, six thousand years ago during the **Cenozoic Era. (Current)**

The creation account according to the first three verses of Genesis 1 occurred as three different events that took place in four different eras of the earth's history. It should not be considered as one event. We miss the mark for all these ages by grouping all three verses into one creation account. The time frame between Genesis 1:1 and Genesis 1:2 is approximately 4.5 billion years minus sixty-five million years.

Scientifically, the age of the universe is estimated to be 13.8 billion, and the earth is 4.5 billion years. It is true that the God who created the universe is eternal and He existed before Genesis 1:1 according to the theological account from the Bible.

Revelation 4:8...which was and is and is to come.

When Moses asked God, "What is Your name?"

"And God said unto Moses, 'I Am That I Am,' and He said, 'Thus shalt thou say unto the children of Israel, I Am hath sent me unto you'" (Exodus 3:14).

"'I am Alpha and Omega, the beginning and the ending,' saith the Lord, which is, and which was, and which is to come, the Almighty" (Revelation 1:8).

First Creation

Genesis 1:1—In the beginning, God created the heaven and the earth.

Universe—Uni means single and verse means spoken sentence.

In the beginning—Does not give us the exact date. According to the scientific evidence it is between 13.8 to 4.5 billion years ago. Just for our understanding with time, let us consider the earth's age as 4.5 billion years.

God—The God Almighty known as "YAHWEH," Elohim, or Adonai the Supreme God. The God who is known in the Hebrew and Christian Bible simply as the Living God.

Created—To bring into existence, something out of nothing. Time, space, and matter came into existence at the same time.

Heaven—Known as sky where the birds fly and clouds form. The sun, moon, planets, and the stars are situated just above that, including galaxies beyond galaxies.

Earth—The home for the plants and living creatures, and it is a planet with land surface and soil. The earth was created during the Precambrian Era.

How did God create the universe 4.5 billion years ago?

The Bible does not give us the exact account of how God began His creation. However, the scripture gives us some clue in Proverbs 3:19–20, "The LORD by wisdom hath founded the earth; by understanding hath He established the heavens." By His knowledge, the depths are broken up, and the clouds drop down the dew.

The Creator possessed with great knowledge and deep wisdom (Proverbs 8:22–31), had a well-planned design to create the universe. Considering the vital elements that form the universe, we can predict Genesis 1:1. In the beginning, God created the heaven and the earth. God created the tiny objects called atoms (with subatomic particles), which is the smallest unit of ordinary matter that forms chemical elements. God designed the atom and placed the information code in it. There are 118 known elements, and some are yet to be discovered. God set these atoms in motion, thus space, time, and matter came into existence after taking its course. After its formation, the universe looked beautiful as you see today. The creation of the atom along with the laws of physics, etc. was one of the greatest creations of God that brought the universe into existence.

Proof of the Age of the Earth at the Precambrian Era at the First Creation

Dating: More than seventy meteorites that have fallen to earth have had their ages calculated by radiometric dating. The oldest of these are dated 4.5 billion years, and the formation of the rocks took place about 4.5 billion years ago.

In the first creation, God created heaven or sky according to Genesis 1:1, which looked like what we see today with the naked eye. He also created the sun to rule the day, the moon and the twinkling stars to rule the night. As we know today, the solar system existed during that time. The sun's presence and the earth rotation created days consisting of twenty-four hours and 365 days in a year. It also resulted in the creation of the seasons because the earth was rotating on its tilted axis and around the sun like today.

Also, when God created the universe, He created gravitation, the electromagnetic field, and weak interaction and strong interaction principles which are the laws of the universe fine-tuned for life on earth. God is the creator of gravity, and still scientists are yet to come up with the exact meaning of gravity. We know that there is a mathematical calculation to know gravity without knowing what it is but how it behaves. God created laws of physics, relativity, electromagnetic fields, etc. to support and sustain His creation.

After the cooling of the earth, God started His creative work. The features of the earth remained the same for years with the ocean on top, crust, asthenosphere, mantle, outer core, and inner core.

Geological Column

The geological column was put forth by scientists to reveal the different eras and periods of the earth's history. The well-known eras are Precambrian, Paleozoic, Mesozoic and Cenozoic Era.

The Fossil Record Shows Early Creation in the Precambrian Era

Precambrian Era: When the time was appropriate, the first appearance of life was recorded in the Precambrian Era. God created the micro creatures like bacteria and stromatolites. Basically, single celled organisms were existed in this Era.

The Fossil Record Shows Secondary Creation During the Cambrian Period, Paleozoic Era

Paleozoic Era—Cambrian period begins approximately 542 million years ago. The creation account during the Cambrian Period happened around 542 million years ago. It was the first time a major group of animals appeared suddenly in the fossil record that lived in the Cambrian Period. It finds many kinds of animals living on land and sea and different kinds of vegetation found on the earth and in the sea during other periods of Paleozoic Era.

The earth was filled with lush vegetation, and animals roamed on the face of the earth and in deep waters. The fossil record shows that all kinds of rainforest vegetation were present on the land as well as in the sea. Also, God created a few kinds of dinosaurs in this Era.

Mesozoic Era begins approximately 251 million years ago. This era is known as the middle era between the Paleozoic and Cenozoic Era, and it is also known as the age of reptiles and the conifers. Dinosaurs, monstrous beasts, and mammals roamed the earth. Conifers, which included redwood, yews, pines, cypress, and other trees, also existed. The flowering plants also appeared during this Era.

This was the condition of heaven and earth for many years. It was beautiful and full of life. There was dawn and dusk, the sun appeared in the sky every day without fail, the rain brought new life for ages. **God designed His creation and built order, uniformity, and rational into nature.**

End of the Mesozoic Era

The Mesozoic Era ended sixty-five million years ago during the Cretaceous Period, which is the last period in the Mesozoic Era. The prehistoric reptiles known as **dinosaurs** were created during the middle to late Triassic Period of the Mesozoic Era, some 251 million years ago. They were members of a subclass of reptiles called the archosaurs, a group that also includes birds and crocodiles. Dinosaurs lived and roamed on the earth for 186 million years. Then one day, sixty-five million years ago, suddenly, a devastating **asteroid** impacted the earth with a great blow, and dinosaurs and other species became extinct from the face of the earth.

The Catastrophic Event of an Asteroid

There is scientific evidence that shows an asteroid crashed to the earth with high velocity. The size of the asteroid was said to be 6 to 9 miles wide, and the earth was impacted beyond recognition. Fire rained from the sky; there were volcanic eruptions and heat increased to high levels. There is scientific evidence that shows the rocks folded to its side, and all living creatures and plants were wiped out, including dinosaurs.

So, we can conclude that the earth was approximately 4.5 billion minus 65 million years old. Plants and animals existed for many years in the first creation, and the asteroid brought death and destruction to all the living creatures, including plants sixty-five million years ago prior to Genesis 1:2. There is geological evidence that shows the end of the Mesozoic Era and the beginning of the present Cenozoic Era, which is called the **KT boundary** known as Cretaceous and Tertiary boundary.

It is the thin dark/gray line one inch to three inches in size seen in all continents, and it contains clay and minerals like iridium. Iridium is a very rare element found in the earth's crust, and high concentrations in this layer show that the asteroid crashed to the earth and brought epic proportions of devastation. All three eras, Precambrian, Paleozoic and Mesozoic, came to an end due to this destruction.

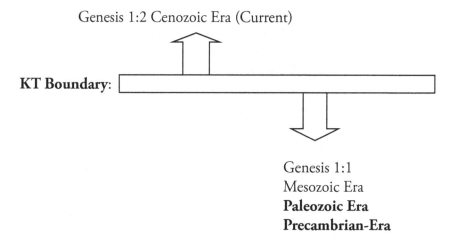

Basically, the first creation according to Genesis 1:1 came to an end with the loss of living and nonliving things on the face of the earth. Genesis 1:1 and 1:2 gives us approximately 4.5 billion years.

Gen: 1:2—The Silent Years of the Earth and the Sun for 65 Million Years: The Beginning of the Tertiary Period, Cenozoic Era

Genesis 1:2 says that the earth was without form and void and the darkness was upon the face of the deep. And the Spirit of God moved upon the face of the waters.

Let us explore in detail the reasons that caused the earth to be without form and void for sixty-five million years.

The earth suffered one of the greatest catastrophic events due to an asteroid. The beautiful earth that once enjoyed perfect balance is undergoing pain with dead life everywhere. The life producing tiny creatures lost their way to death. The living and moving creatures on the land and the seas have now become dead carcasses with no one to bury them. All the living organisms small and big have gone. Sudden death came to this earth without warning.

The God who created the universe was grieving with His creation by moving upon the face of the waters for sixty-five million years. He neither forgot nor ignored His creation even when the earth was without form and void. By covering the earth with water, God protected it from radiation and its effects for sixty-five million years.

The main casualty on the earth is said to be the dinosaurs. The beautiful and magnificent creatures that once roamed the earth and enjoyed life with power and strength were gone. Young and old had no hope of survival; it was not slow but a sudden extinction. The life in deep oceans which once thrived with lush vegetation and coral reefs vanished. The fish and other sea creatures suffered and faced dire consequences when death seemed nowhere close.

Let Us Compare This Event to the Biblical Explanation

Theological explanations found in the Bible gives rise to this theory of the earth being without form and void, why the darkness covered the earth and the effects of an asteroid.

Isaiah 14:12–15, "[12] How art thou fallen from heaven, O Lucifer, son of the morning! How art thou cut down to the ground, which didst weaken the nations! [13] For thou hast said in thine heart, 'I will ascend into heaven. I will exalt my throne above the stars of God. I will sit also upon the mount of the congregation, in the sides of the north. [14] I will ascend above the heights of the clouds. I will be like the Most High.' [15] Yet thou shall be brought down to hell, to the sides of the pit."

This event indicates a huge turn during the first creation. When Lucifer, one of the archangels, rebels against God, there was a battle that took place in heaven, and Lucifer, with his minions, were thrown out of heaven. This story seems just a joke for many people, but it provides a significant correlation with scientific evidence.

This event caused a great impact in the sky, and powers of the universe were shaken. The light and energy-producing objects lost their power. The skies were no longer lit to see the glory and wonders in the universe. The sun and stars were no longer able to dominate the skies. Darkness was everywhere for sixty-five million years. The black out that took place could not be understood or imagined. The sun and the stars remained in the skies as lifeless objects. The heavens that declare the glory of God and the firmament that showed His handiwork became obsolete. The magnificent glory once radiant and visual could not be seen for many years.

At the same time, due to the instability in the sky, the asteroid hit the earth with a great explosion. The earth suffered one of the great disasters in history, and the blow destroyed all ecosystems, including the ozone layer. There was a great explosion causing the magnetic field to rise to its highest levels. Fire raining from the skies increased the temperature, causing the heat to rise to unreliable levels, causing rocks to fold 90 degrees because they lost their hardness and became soft. The unimaginable heat caused the glaciers at the North and South Pole to melt, vaporize, and be thrown in the sky and travel for unknown distances.

Immediately following this event, great amounts of water vapor was thrown into the atmosphere, causing heavy torrential rain amounting in great floods, and the evidence shows ice rain down on the earth. Tsunamis were formed due to earthquakes, these floods brought landslides and mudslides, burying all the living and nonliving things on the face of the earth. Since everything was soft due to the high temperatures, these floods altered the geological features of the earth forever. Some of the visible changes are as follows:

1. **Formation of the Grand Canyon:** It is 277 miles long, 18 miles wide, and a mile deep into the crust of the earth. The erosion by flowing waters carved one of the wonders of nature. Each layer tells the story of the earth. The rocks

found at the bottom of the canyons are 1.8 billion years old.

2. **Kentucky Mammoth Caves**: The caves were formed due to the heavy flow of water for years. It is the world's longest known cave system.

3. **Niagara Falls**: The creation of the falls due to erosion was caused by the flowing of water for many years. There were other waterfalls created in different countries during this period.

4. **Mountains and Valleys**: Shift in plate tectonics caused volcanic eruptions at the earth's crust, creating mountains when the continental plates smashed against each other. Heavy deluge with high velocities carried the soil long distances and deposited it in different locations. This flood formed the mountains and valleys and later water remained on the earth for sixty-five million years according to Genesis 1:2.

The asteroid crash that preceded the prehistoric flood should not be confused with Noah's flood. The following table shows the difference between the two floods:

<u>Prehistoric Flood—Global</u>   <u>Noah's Flood</u>

65 Million Years Ago	4,400 Years Ago
Plants and animals were extinct instantaneously	Noah and his family survived with the animals on the ark, the rest of mankind was destroyed.
Sedimentation of rocks, sand, silt, and lime.	Few fossils found with soft tissue and blood vessels above the KT boundary
Petrified polystrate trees buried quickly	
Plate Tectonic, Continental Drift	
Creation of canyons	
Creation of caves	
Creation of huge craters	

Creation of mountains and valleys	
Quick fossilization of plants and animals below the KT boundary	
Formation of waterfalls due to erosion during the flowing of water	
Iridium found at the KT boundary, shows the end of an era and the beginning of a new era	

The account of Noah's flood is true, but forty days of rain and water staying on the earth for 150 days or even a year would not have created the Grand Canyon or Mount Everest or caused any other major geological changes on the face of the earth. The fossil record from the Paleozoic and Mesozoic Eras is found below the KT boundary, and it is from prehistoric floods that happened during the first creation. All others, like tissue with blood cells found above the KT boundary during the Cenozoic Era, was from Noah's flood and happened during the second creation.

The lack of evidence of human's fossil discredits Noah's flood as a cause for plants and animals' fossil found in the earth crest.

The effects of the flood remained for sixty-five million years exactly according to Genesis 1:2 that the earth was without form and void and the darkness was upon the face of the deep. And the Spirit of God moved upon the face of the waters.

The earth was dormant for many years, just digesting the shock, pain, and tremors for years. During this period, the earth produced coal and oil due to the billions of trees and animals buried during the flood.

The scientific evidence shows that the earth went through an ice age for a while during this Cenozoic Era due to cooler temperatures and then again when temperatures increased. Water covered the earth according to Genesis 1:2 to protect it from radiation and its harmful effects for sixty-five million years. **During these silent years of the earth, there was no activity found in the earth strata for sixty-five million years.**

Before this catastrophe, the earth's surface was flat, meaning there were no mountains or valleys, no hills or gorges. The condition of the earth covered with water remained for sixty-five million years and it was fresh water not saltwater. This brought new geological features on the surface of the earth. There was a blackout in the sky for the same duration.

Genesis 1:3—The Second Creation/Rearranging in Six Days, Six Thousand Years Ago during the Quaternary Period, Cenozoic Era

I want to bring your attention to one of the biggest discoveries in the creation account. Notice that the earth existed before day 1 of creation according to Genesis 1:3. If the solid earth existed under the waters, then the solar system was in operational mode. We know that without the solar system, the earth cannot stay on its axis and go around the sun in its orbit. That means that both the sun and the earth existed before day 1, but the condition of the sun was dark with no light in it according to Genesis 1:2.

I want to ask you a question, during the six days of creation, on which day was the solid earth created? The answer is none. God never created the solid earth a second time. There is no second or third earth; one earth existed from the beginning with the original creation according to Genesis 1:1 for 4.5 billion years. Many before me assumed that the first three verses of Genesis chapter one is interconnected with the creation account. It is not interconnected, rather all three verses have different timelines as I mentioned earlier.

What is the reason for the second creation?

I was contemplating why God is creating a second time when His creation is in an obsolete state. While our attitude may be to let it go, God values His creation, and He has a purpose. God created the beautiful universe once and filled the earth with life. The answer lies in, Isaiah 45:18, "'For thus,' saith the Lord that created the heavens, God Himself that formed the earth and made it. He hath established it. He created it not in vain, **and He formed it to be inhabited**, 'I am the LORD; and there is none else.'"

This is the heart of God; He values every creature He created with wisdom and knowledge. This very reason gave rise to God creating/rearranging the earth a second time six thousand years ago when the earth was lying lifeless and the Spirit of God was grieving and moaning for the loss of His creation by moving on the face of the waters.

Day 1 of the Second Creation/Rearranging

Genesis 1:3–5, "³And God said, 'Let there be light' and there was light. ⁴And God saw the light, that it was good, and God divided the light from the darkness. ⁵And God called the light day, and the darkness He called night. And the evening and the morning were the first day."

God started the second creation six thousand years ago; He created the light. This light I will call a soft light as it is different from the sun's light because there is no piercing power in it, and it has no energy. You can notice it during dawn, dusk, and when the sky is covered with thick black clouds during the rain. This soft light can move and spread everywhere, but sunlight moves straight and cannot be bent. Shadows are clearly visible with the sunlight but not so much with the soft light. So, with this creation of light, God separated the darkness, and He called it day. Thus, the night and day began on the first day, and it was twenty-four hours. (The earth's twenty-four-hour cycle existed from the first creation according to Genesis 1:1).

Day 2 of the Second Creation

Genesis 1: 6–8, "⁶And God said, 'Let there be a firmament in the midst of the waters, and let it divide the waters from the waters.' ⁷And God made the firmament, and divided the waters which were under the firmament from the waters which were above the firmament, and it was so. ⁸And God called the firmament heaven. And the evening and the morning were the second day."

These verses look so simple and unimpressive, but in these verses lies one of the greatest creations, which is still a mystery, and its origin was unknown to man until this book reveals the secret.

The Origin of the Ozone Layer

So, during the second day of creation, God created the sky/firmament by dividing the waters from the waters (Genesis 1:6). By dividing the waters, God created the sky/firmament, the place where birds can fly, and the formation of the clouds takes place.

Creation of the Ozone Layer: The Condition
of the Earth at Genesis 1:2

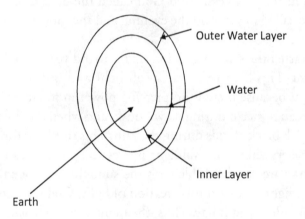

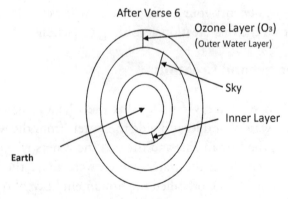

Here in verse 6, God divided the waters which covered the earth into two parts. The outer water layer was pushed outwardly, creating a space called sky/firmament between earth and the outer water layer. During this operation, this body of water became the ozone layer when hydrogen evaporated due to heat and friction, leaving a single molecule of oxygen, and this single oxygen molecule (O) combined with atmospheric oxygen (O_2), thus forming the ozone layer (O_3) whose main function is to protect the earth from the sun's UV rays. Remember that the old ozone layer which was protecting the earth in the first creation was destroyed during the catastrophic event of the asteroid. The sky looks blue due to the sun's rays entering through the ozone layer.

The water, which was under the sky, that is the inner water layer later became seas (Genesis 1:9), thus the second day came into existence.

Day 3 of the Second Creation

Genesis 1:9–10, "⁹And God said, 'Let the waters under the heaven be gathered together unto one place, and let the dryland appear,' and it was so. ¹⁰And God called the dryland earth and the gathering together of the waters He called seas, and God saw that it was good."

Genesis 1:11–13, "¹¹And God said, 'Let the earth bring forth grass, the herb yielding seed, and the fruit tree yielding fruit after his kind, whose seed is in itself, upon the earth,' and it was so. ¹²And the earth brought forth grass and herb yielding seed after his kind, and the tree yielding fruit, whose seed was in it after his kind. and God saw that it was good. ¹³And the evening and the morning were the third day."

So, during the third day, God created the dryland by gathering the water together (inner water layer), thus He created the seas. For ages, mankind believed that the creation of the seas and the appearance of dryland was connected to the creation of the earth. No, it is not. It is just a rearranging of the earth after the asteroid disaster. As water receded from the land, the rivers and creeks were formed on the dryland.

So, during the third day, the Lord God said, let the earth bring forth the grass, herb yielding seed, and fruit trees after his kind. Thus, the grass, the vegetation and the trees started growing except herb yielding plants. Notice here that God never created the seed for grass and the roots for trees because it already existed from the first creation. Since the water covered the face of the earth for years, nothing grew.

Here we have to realize that the growth of vegetation took place not only at the location where God was creating but in all continents, wherever the dryland appeared. The vegetation and trees had free reign of growth for 1,800 years before humans entered the continents after the tower of Babel event. These are the examples that vegetation started growing six thousand years ago:

1. **Methuselah the Bristlecone pine tree**: It is the oldest tree discovered to be five thousand years old, which is in Inyo National Forest in California, and it appeared in the second creation.
2. **The Corel Reef in Australia**: The newly found coral reef in Australia is said to be 4,300 years old, and the oldest coral reef from the first creation disappeared during the catastrophe of the asteroid crashing into the earth.
3. **The Sahara Desert**: It is said to be 4,400 years old. It was formed after Noah's flood during the second creation and covered the thick vegetation which was created during the third day.

Day 4 of the Second Creation

Genesis 1:14–19, "14And God said, 'Let there be lights in the firmament of the heaven to divide the day from the night, and let them be for signs and for seasons and for days and years, 15and let them be for lights in the firmament of the heaven to give light upon the earth,' and it was so. 16And God made two great lights: the greater light to rule the day and the lesser light to rule the night. He made the stars also. [17]And God set them in the firmament of the heaven to give light upon the earth, [18]and to rule over the day and over the night and to divide the light from the darkness, and God saw that it was good. [19]And the evening and the morning were the fourth day."

During the fourth day of creation, the sun, moon, and stars were not created new, rather the Lord God ignited the sun and the stars with fire and with the right amount of power and energy to give light because there was a blackout for sixty-five million years. I gave the account of the earth being covered with darkness, and it shows the absence of light from the sun. That is the reason God had to light the sun to sustain the vegetation, which He created on the third day. The sun is the main energy source for the earth. God created the photosynthesis process for vegetation to survive. Sunlight gives vitamin D for the animals and humans, who were created on the fifth and sixth day. Note: The soft light which was created on day one is very much noticeable throughout the day in the absence of sun due to clouds formation during rain/snow and vice versa. It is not noticeable during the day due to sunlight being more powerful than soft light.

Existence of Comets: The life of comets is said to be ten thousand years. How then are they still in the sky? Since the sun had blacked out for sixty-five million years and the second creation is only six thousand years old, comets still exist.

The fine-tuning and the restoration of the sun took place on the fourth day, six thousand years ago. God ignited the sun and the stars to its previous glory with the right power and energy to sustain life on the earth. After the fine-tuning of the sun, the ice started to form slowly on the North and South Pole and covered the thick vegetation, which was created on day three. God brought forth vegetation on all continents, including North and South Pole, wherever dryland appeared. For this reason, thick vegetation is found under the glaciers at North and South pole.

Now, we can answer many of the unanswered questions which scientists were seeking about the restoration of the sun's energy.

1. Why is the light from farther stars has not been reached the earth yet when it is traveling approximately 186,282 miles/second and earth is 4.5 billion years old?

    The right answer is, there was a blackout in the sky for sixty-five million years, and the stars were reignited during second creation on day four, six thousand years ago.
2. The loss of energy by the sun every minute should have caused the sun to lose its power when it is approximately 4.5 billion years old?

    According to second creation, the sun was reignited and restored on day four, six thousand years ago. That is the reason the sun is operating with potential power to sustain the life on the earth.

Day 5 of the Second Creation

Genesis 1:20–23, "²⁰And God said, 'Let the waters bring forth abundantly the moving creature that hath life and fowl that may fly above the earth in the open firmament of heaven.' ²¹And God created great whales and every living creature that moveth, which the waters brought forth abundantly, after their kind, and every winged fowl after his kind, and God saw that it was good. ²²And God blessed them, saying, 'Be fruitful and multiply and fill the waters in the seas, and let fowl multiply in the earth.' ²³And the evening and the morning were the fifth day."

So, God created many kinds of sea creatures and many kinds of birds in the air. Some of the sea creatures are the same as in the first creation, and some are newly created. The size of these creatures is smaller compared to the Paleozoic and Mesozoic Era, except the whales (Genesis 1:21). The blue whale, which was created during the second creation, is bigger in size compared to dinosaurs. For example, the story of Jonah being in the belly of a fish is true. Thousands of species which were created during the first creation are missing in the second creation. The sharks reappeared in the second creation and dominated the ocean and the seas.

These sea creatures sprung up in all oceans, seas, and in rivers according to the weather conditions and ecosystems.

Even the birds were created in all continents according to the natural weather patterns. God knows what is best for His creation.

In Genesis 1:20, I want to bring your attention to the firmament which was created on the second day of creation and is mentioned here. "And fowl that may fly above the earth in the open firmament of heaven." The space created by God by moving the outer water layer above the earth created the space for birds to fly, and eventually, the waters became the ozone layer.

God blessed them and said to be fruitful and multiply. These two characters, "fruitful and multiply," dominated His creation.

Even the stars in the universe have been multiplying since the first creation, which was 4.5 billion years ago. It is estimated that two hundred billion galaxies exist at the present time. The Bible says in Isaiah 51:13 that God stretched the heavens.

Day 6 of the Second Creation

Genesis 1:24–31, "²⁴And God said, 'Let the earth bring forth the living creature after his kind, cattle and creeping thing and beast of the earth after his kind,' and it was so. ²⁵And God made the beast of the earth after his kind and cattle after their kind and everything that creepeth upon the earth after his kind, and God saw that it was good. ²⁶And God said, 'Let us make man in Our image, after Our likeness and let them have dominion over the fish of the sea and over the fowl of the air and over the cattle and over all the earth and over every creeping thing that creepeth upon the earth.' ²⁷So, God created man in His own image, in the image of God created He him, male and female created He them. ²⁸And God blessed them, and God said unto them, 'Be fruitful and multiply and replenish the earth and subdue it and have dominion over the fish of the sea and over the fowl of the air and over every living thing that moveth upon the earth.' ²⁹And God said, 'Behold, I have given you every herb-bearing seed, which is upon the face of all the earth and every tree, in the which is the fruit of a tree-yielding seed. To you it shall be for meat. [30]And to every beast of the earth and to every fowl of the air and to everything that creepeth upon the earth, wherein there is life, I have given every green herb for meat,' and it was so. [31]And God saw everything that He had made, and, behold, it was very good. And the evening and the morning were the sixth day."

So, on the sixth day, God created different kinds of animals on the land; some of them existed during the first creation. And God said to replenish the earth because the first creation was destroyed during the asteroid catastrophe. Notice that the dinosaurs were missing in the second creation due to their dominance and aggressiveness.

At the command of the Lord God Almighty, the earth brought forth the animals according to its kind. This event did not take place in a particular location rather throughout the earth in all continents simultaneously wherever there was dryland. It was created male and female to adapt to the weather conditions and ecosystems on land and to grow and multiply. Different kinds of apes, monkeys, gorillas, predators, such as big cats, and prowling predators and mammals etc. appeared on the face of the earth. These animals multiplied in all continents 1,800 years before the human placed his foot on these continents. Humans started moving out from the Mesopotamia region after the event of the tower of Babel and found that vegetation and animals existed in those regions.

> And God said, Let us make man in our image, after our likeness: and let them have dominion over the fish of the sea, and over the fowl of the air, and over the cattle, over all the earth, and over every creeping thing that creepeth upon the earth. So God created man in His own image, in the image of God created he him, male and female created he them. And God blessed them, and God said unto them, be fruitful, and multiply, and replenish the earth, and subdue it: and have dominion over the fish of the sea,

and over the fowl of the air, and over every living thing that moveth upon the earth. (Genesis
1:26–28)

In Genesis 1:26, God decided to make man in His own image
and in His likeness. The purpose is to dominate and take care of His
creation.

In Genesis 1:27, God created man in His own image, "In the
image of God created He him, male and female created He them."

In Genesis 1:28, God blessed them and said to be fruitful and
multiply. These two characters, fruitful and multiply, dominated His
creation. God created plants, animals, and humans with the same
theory, fruitful and multiply.

I want to clarify the misconception regarding the following
Bible verse:

Mark 10:6, "But from the beginning of the creation, God made
them male and female." Here, Jesus is not speaking of Adam and Eve,
rather about His first creation. The creation account from Genesis
1:1 is His first creation before the asteroid disaster. He created animals on the land and sea during the Paleozoic and Mesozoic Era. He
created them male and female. That is what Jesus is talking about,
not Adam and Eve.

Genesis 1:29–30, "And God said, 'Behold, I have given you
every herb-bearing seed, which is upon the face of all the earth and
every tree, in the which is the fruit of a tree-yielding seed. To you it
shall be for meat. 30And to every beast of the earth and to every fowl
of the air and to everything that creepeth upon the earth, wherein
there is life, I have given every green herb for meat,' and it was so."

God gave the blueprint of a perfect diet that contains carbohy-
drates, green leaves, meat (later), and fruits.

Why is the account for the first creation missing according to
Genesis 1:1 while we have a detailed account of the second creation
according to Genesis 1:3?

It was because Adam was not created during the first creation,
and it was only animals and plants during Genesis 1:1. That is the
reason why we have no account of the first creation, but we have a

six-day second creation account because Adam was created, and the information was passed on to his next subsequent generations.

Day 7: God rested on the seventh day, thus it is a Holy Sabbath day (Genesis 2:1–3).

Chapter Two

———— ⚬ ————

Who Is the Creator in Genesis 1:1?

The first three words which appeared in Genesis 1:1, "In the beginning," reappeared after 4.5 billion plus, four thousand years in the gospel of John 1:1. This time, it did not give us the account of creation rather the Creator Himself.

John 1:1–3, "¹In the beginning was the Word and the Word was with God and the Word was God. ²The same was in the beginning with God. ³All things were made by Him, and without Him was not anything made that was made."

Here is the biblical explanation about the Creator who created the universe in the beginning; it also explains briefly about the structure of the living God. God in the Bible appeared as three in one known as the triune God. It is as follows:

God the Father—Plans
God the Son—Executes (Implements)
God the Holy Spirit—Empowers

All three are one with different functions. When God the father planned to create the universe, it was His Son, Jesus Christ, who implemented it by creating tiny objects called atom/atoms and set it in motion and created the first creation in Genesis 1:1; later, His second creation includes Adam and Eve.

The work of the Holy Spirit was to empower and authenticate every aspect of creation which the Son of God created. Basically, the Holy Spirit has to issue the certificate of occupancy called (C of O) by placing His seal of approval.

When Adam and Eve sinned against the Creator, they were thrown out of the garden of Eden, thus sin, curse, and death entered the human race. God was grieved and planned to redeem mankind by sending His Son as a redeemer. We see His famous statement in the Bible.

John 3:16, "For God so loved the world that He gave His only begotten Son, that whosoever believeth in Him should not perish but have everlasting life."

Why Jesus?

God the Son created the universe with His wisdom and knowledge and designed the complicated atom to create the universe, space, time, and matter. Jesus created the cell which is unique in its formation and contains 3.5 billion genetic codes, the language and information to create a new life on the earth. Jesus, who is the Creator, carried the burden of the redemption of His human creation on His shoulder.

For four thousand years before Christ, people were looking forward for a Messiah, the one to come on this earth to free them from bondage. Every heart knows that they have sinned against the living God. The Bible says in, Romans 3:23, "For all have sinned and come short of the glory of God."

Also, there was a prophecy written in the book of Isaiah around seven hundred years before Jesus came to this world. Isaiah 9:6, "For unto us a child is born, unto us a son is given, and the government shall be upon His shoulder, and His name shall be called wonderful, counselor, the mighty God, the everlasting Father, the Prince of Peace."

When the time was right, the Son of God, who is your Creator, left the glory of Heaven, came to this earth, and was born through the Virgin Mary. His name is Jesus, the Lamb of God who takes away the sins of this world.

It looks impossible for us even to think that the virgin can conceive and bear a child. But it happened naturally by the supernatural power of God. When Jesus was born, He was human and God at the same time. One simple explanation is that it was Jesus who created the life on earth by designing a cell and placing the codes in it. He has the power and authority to change the code of a cell supernaturally. The Holy Spirit empowered the birth of Jesus. Every miracle you see in the Bible is literal because it is done in the natural with supernatural intervention.

How God can do the miracles in the natural?

When God created the universe with life on earth, He placed the written code in it, and He alone has the power to lock and unlock it. The living cell for example contains 3.5 billion codes written in it. Every human being and animal have a unique combination of codes; that is the reason every human fingerprint is different, and no two zebra stripes are the same. Let us examine Jesus's statement.

In Luke 12:7, He said, "But even the very hairs of your head are all numbered. Fear not therefore ye are of more value than many sparrows."

How God can claim this is because He alone knows the combination of your genetic code and knows the number of hair that code generates on your head. He knows the color of your eyes because of the same reason.

Jesus was born in a manger, grew up in a place called Nazareth in Israel, and preached the kingdom of God to multitudes who were looking for the Messiah. Jesus performed many miracles; He healed the sick, delivered those oppressed by evil spirits, and preached the good news.

When Jesus healed the sick, people around Him were surprised by the overflowing power of God through Him. The blind could see, the lame could walk, and leprosy was healed. Jesus could do miracles by correcting the defects in the genetic codes because He is the author and creator of genetic codes.

Even nature heard His voice and obeyed. He calmed the raging seas. The disciples also acknowledged that even the wind and the sea obey.

Matthew 8:23–27, "²³And when He was entered into a ship, His disciples followed Him. ²⁴And, behold, there arose a great tempest in the sea, insomuch that the ship was covered with the waves, but He was asleep. ²⁵And His disciples came to Him and awoke Him, saying, 'Lord, save us, we perish.' ²⁶And He saith unto them, 'Why are ye fearful, O ye of little faith?' Then He arose and rebuked the winds and the sea, and there was a great calm. ²⁷But the men marveled, saying, 'What manner of man is this that even the winds and the sea obey Him!'"

Jesus could do miracles in nature because He is the creator and author of every law in the universe. He created and laid the earth's foundation not by bricks, stones, or even concrete but by an unseen law called gravity. Newton found the mathematical equation for gravitational force centuries ago, which later helped Americans to put astronauts on the moon.

What about the wind? Nobody can define the exact meaning of the wind, but they explain the effects of the wind through the atmospheric pressure formula.

This Creator came for us to save us from death, but He was falsely accused, beaten, and finally He was hanged on the cross for our sin.

Isaiah 53:3–7, "³He is despised and rejected of men, a man of sorrows, and acquainted with grief, and we hid as it were our faces from Him. He was despised, and we esteemed Him not. ⁴Surely He hath borne our griefs and carried our sorrows, yet we did esteem Him stricken, smitten of God, and afflicted. ⁵But He was wounded for our transgressions. He was bruised for our iniquities. The chastisement of our peace was upon Him, and with His stripes we are healed. ⁶All we like sheep have gone astray. We have turned everyone to his own way, and the LORD hath laid on Him the iniquity of us all. ⁷He was oppressed, and He was afflicted, yet He opened not His mouth. He is brought as a lamb to the slaughter, and as a sheep before her shearers is dumb, so He opened not His mouth."

This is the very purpose that God the Father sent His Son to die on the cross for the remission of our sins. He shed every drop of His blood and died and was buried. Why is the blood important?

Because life is in the blood. On the third day, He was raised by the power of the Holy Spirit. Because Jesus was resurrected, we have the hope that one day we will rise from our death and be with Him in Glory, that is the blessed hope that Jesus assures to everyone who believes in Him. It is known as being born again or saved from sin.

Jesus said, "I am the way the truth and the life, no one comes to the Father but by Me."

Romans 10:9, "That if you confess with your mouth the Lord Jesus and believe in your heart that God has raised Him from the dead, you will be saved."

Also, you will have hope of eternal life as a free gift.

Romans 6:23, "For the wages of sin is death, but the gift of God is eternal life through Jesus Christ our Lord."

Everyone who repents and asks God for forgiveness of their sins will receive forgiveness and become a new creation in Jesus Christ.

The Bible also says that at the end of time, Jesus will come a second time to judge the living and the dead. Hebrew 9:27 says, "And as it is appointed unto men once to die but after this the judgment."

When Jesus comes back to judge the earth, there will be a blackout again in the universe.

Matthew 24:29, "Immediately after the tribulation of those days shall the sun be darkened and the moon shall not give her light and the stars shall fall from heaven, and the powers of the heavens shall be shaken."

When the new heaven and earth comes, everyone who is saved will be rejoicing in heaven where there is no sorrow and there is no pain.

I urge everyone to know and understand that the God of the Bible is also known as the God of science.

Chapter Three

———— ⌘ ————

Darwin's Theory of Evolution
Is a Myth and a Lie

L ife on earth did not evolve, but it was created. Since we found the
Maker who made the watch and connected the dots to eliminate
the gaps, it is time to dismantle the evolution theory.

The battle of minds raging to dominate the cultures, societies,
and nations among scientists, philosophers, and theologians is not a
new phenomenon, it happens in every generation.

The naturalists and materialists believe that material and energy
came together at the big bang to create the universe but failed to
produce the origin of matter and the source of energy.

If evolution was involved at the time of creation, this universe
would not have been formed with all the principles evolving for centuries. On the other hand, the life on earth never evolved, the scientific evidence does not support it.

The Cambrian explosion poses a challenge to evolution. The
sudden appearance of species in the Cambrian explosion was a great
surprise for scientists because fully formed animals appeared in fossil
records. The Precambrian layer does not show any sign of developing
life in the strata.

The life on earth did not generate from the primordial soup
theory. The theory was put to test in the labs but did not produce the
desired results.

Darwin stated that "if my theory be true, numberless intermediate varieties…most assuredly have existed." It is well-known as a missing link never found in the earth's history. Fossil records in the Cambrian explosion show that many kinds of animals abruptly appeared on the scene, but the Precambrian strata does not show any existence of animals, which were neither in transition nor fully grown.

Dr. Stephen J. Gould said, "The absence of fossil evidence for intermediary stages has been a persistent and nagging problem for evolution."

Darwin's theory indicates cosmic evolution. The creation of space, time, and matter would not have taken place if it were not instantaneous. The laws of gravity did not evolve, and the chain reaction of the atom would not have taken place with precision. The chemical, organic, and macroevolution never happened.

Microevolution—Variations within the kinds takes place all the time due to mutations in the cell within the kinds. For example, all my three children differ in looks and stature. Mutation of cells never produced different kinds of animals. That is debunked because the cell cannot produce a different kind other than its own.

The primordial soup cannot produce any species nor did the hominid, which is designated as the apes living in the wooded area never produced humans. The cells of the hominids produced the same kind of hominids, not humans.

Humans are created in the image of God and can achieve greater things that no other animals can achieve. Image of God means that we have the body, soul/mind, and spirit. That is why we can reason with many ideas, and those ideas can be transferred through the brain to the body to produce the result. It is like a technology written with the help of science that technology was later transferred to AutoCAD sent to a machine to produce a tool. The brain is the catalyst to pass/observe the information between the mind and the body. We can lead a productive and meaningful life because we are created in the likeness of God. The idea generated as a thought can produce new inventions in every area of human life, which animals cannot do.

When God created the living beings, He designed the magnificent and complex cell to produce its own kind. This cell is like a factory and has 3.5 billion genetic codes hidden in it. It has the information to produce its own kind, and it cannot produce any other kind. Evolution never gives us absolute answers, rather it only speculates. Life never originated by chance, but it was God's creation.

Dr. Tour argues that the cell cannot be replicated in the lab, and it cannot produce a different kind other than its own kind.

Dr. Berlinski argues that if any changes are made at the beginning to the cell, it will destroy it, and if any changes are made later, the growth of a species has already been in the process of formation.

Evolution argues about adaptation. Adaptation is a God-given ability placed in all living beings. We know how to adapt and survive. Darwin's theory remains as a theory because no one knows how it really works.

Charles Darwin admitted in 1859, "Geology assuredly does not reveal any such finely graduated organic chain, and this, perhaps, is the most obvious and serious objection which can be urged against the theory. The explanation lies, as I believe, in the extreme imperfection of geological records."

At one point, Darwin was frustrated and started blaming the geological records for not proving his evolution theory. Moreover, all the living creatures were destroyed sixty-five million years ago, and the evolution theory came to an end abruptly. It is time to reconsider whether it is doing justice to mankind if we do not dismantle it.

Chapter Four

---- ✺ ----

An Invitation to Discover from the Creator Himself

A t the end of chapter 2, I stated that the God of the Bible is the God of science. The God who created the heaven and the earth according to Genesis 1:1, and the God, who created humans in the second creation, is inviting all mankind to discover the truth and laws of nature hidden in the universe.

The great philosopher and king, Solomon, said in Proverbs 25:2, "It is the glory of God to conceal a matter, and it is the glory of kings to search it out."

The God of the universe is inviting human beings to explore the secrets of the universe. God has laid all the laws in His creation and is not afraid of attempts made by humans to reveal the secrets hidden in the nature.

The conflict between science and faith is futile, and the fight between science and religion is a waste of time. Faith and science should go hand in hand because the God who created the universe is the God of science, and scientific evidence must prove its origin. There are pseudoscientists and pseudoscientific evidence that exists, and we should be aware of it. According to my knowledge, most of the scientists who discovered new things the hard way was honest in their findings. It is not easy to discover something without a painstaking process, and it does not always guarantee the desired results.

Many early scientists believed in their Creator during their quest to discover. For example, Galileo found that the sun is the center of our universe and the earth revolves around the sun, which was against the religious belief of his time. Others like Johannes Kepler, Robert Boil, and Sir Isaac Newton and many others had reverence for God.

Many times when we see death and suffering, we tend to think that God is not interfering with His creation and He is probably not interested in it. But the truth of the matter is that may be right when it comes to nature because He has created such a magnificent system which is self-sustainable for ages, but when it comes to mankind, God is very much involved with His creation. I want to explore two reasons that He is still active with His creation when it comes to mankind.

First, He is a Sovereign God, and He can pass His judgment and involve His creation as He wishes any time and any place.

Genesis 18:20–21, "²⁰And the LORD said, 'Because the cry of Sodom and Gomorrah is great and because their sin is very grievous, ²¹ I will go down now and see whether they have done altogether according to the cry of it, which is come unto me, and if not, I will know.'"

God's judgment fell on these two cities, and He destroyed it by sulfur or brimstone.

The flood during Noah's time was God's judgment that destroyed all human beings except Noah and his family.

The second reason is when the cry of a human being rises to His throne, it causes His hand to move and get involved in His creation. He is the God who hears and answers all our prayers/petitions according to the riches and glory in His Son, Jesus Christ.

Here are some examples from the Bible: Psalms 34:17, **"The *righteous* cry and the Lord heareth and delivereth them out of all their troubles."** Romans 10:13, **"For whosoever shall call upon the name of the Lord shall be saved."**

When the children of Israel cried unto the Lord, Moses was sent by God to free them from their slavery and bondage and set them free.

It makes it easier for humans to understand the things of God if they have an encounter with their Creator. The science will never disprove God because without God, there is no science. There are numerous things to explore, such as how all the miracles mentioned in the Bible went against the laws of nature.

Jesus and Peter walking on the water literally happened. How is this possible? Jesus is the Creator of water and knows the buoyancy law. The water can lift huge cruise ships; therefore, why not our weight?

Jesus turning water into wine literally happened because the Bible says so. He could change the chemical composition of water to wine because He is the Creator of water and wine and wrote the codes in it.

Explore the power of your eyesight which is faster than the speed of light. The stars which are billions of miles away can be captured by your eyesight in a fraction of a second. That is how marvelously we are created.

What about your imagination and thought process?

It shows that the Creator has all the authority over His creation. Let us know and understand the Creator who created the heaven and the earth through His power.

CPSIA information can be obtained
at www.ICGtesting.com
Printed in the USA
BVHW031527151221
624016BV00008B/764